Huggy's New Coats

Wendy Rigg

Huggy didn't feel well.

He had lots of aches and pains and he felt very tired.

Sheena Sheep's little lambs said:

We have some new paints." "No thank you," said Huggy.

He didn't even feel like hanging upside down with Brenda Bat's babies.

Harold Horse asked him if he'd like a gallop around the field on his back;

"Come for a ride on my back, Huggy!"

But no, he was too tired.

Manjit Mouse said maybe Huggy would like to play a quieter game; how about marbles with his children. "No thanks," said a tired Huggy.

Huggy decided to go and have a little lie down – then perhaps he might feel better.

Mummy was worried. It wasn't like her little boy to want to go to bed before bedtime, or to be too tired to play with his friends.

Dr Raj looked at Huggy over the top of his big round specs.
"I think we'll give you a little blood test, Huggy."
Huggy was very brave and nurse Kerrie gave him a sweet.

Huggy had to go to hospital every day for six weeks for some special medicine to make him feel better. Nurse Kerrie was always pleased to see him as he was one of her favourites.

At the hospital, Huggy could choose his lunch from one of the pictures that nurse Kerrie showed him. Usually worm pie was his favourite, but sometimes he fancied snails on toast. Some days Huggy didn't feel like eating anything so nurse Kerrie gave him a glass of milk.

What meal would you choose?

Huggy met lots of other children at the hospital. Sometimes after their special medicine they would play in the playroom for a little while.

Huggy liked the Lego best, but sometimes when he felt especially tired or poorly he would curl up on mummy's lap with his thumb in his mouth and have a story.

After a little while of visits to the hospital,
something strange started to happen;
some of Huggy's spines started to fall out!

Dr Raj told Huggy that this usually happens with the special medicine, but they would grow back afterwards.

Huggy looked in the mirror every day to see how many spines he had left. One day when he looked, they had all fallen out. This made Huggy feel a bit chilly, but he thought that he looked rather like a smooth smart dude! Mummy said that he would have to wear a warm jumper all the time to stop him feeling cold.

Huggy's animal friends had a good idea.
Brenda Bat said: "I have some soft green moss in my tree home Huggy.
It will make a smart coat for you." Brenda and her babies worked all night,
and in the morning the moss coat was ready.

Huggy tried it on.
The coat was thick, soft and green, with big buttons made from the bark
of Brenda's tree. It was a tiny bit damp, and there were a few
insects hiding in the moss, this was a bonus for Huggy
(hedgehogs like to eat insects).

"Yum, scrummy, delicious,"
he thought as he chomped on a shiny black beetle.

"I bet no one else has a coat that you can eat!"

Huggy wore his coat out in the sun. It was very smart but unfortunately as the sun shone down, the moss began to dry out and started to fall apart.

Huggy was sad because he really liked his moss coat.
"Poor you," said Sarah Silkworm. "Never mind, I'll make you a beautiful cloak from some of my silk."

She then set about spinning lots of creamy silk, which she then made into a soft stylish cloak. Huggy wrapped it around himself; he thought that he looked like Superman. The cloak was lovely but that night when he snuggled down in bed with his brother and sister, their spines tangled up in the delicate material and made holes in the silk. They were both very sorry, but after a few days there was hardly anything left of the silk cloak.

I look like Superman - up, up and away!

"Don't worry Huggy," said Sheena Sheep.
"What you need is some of my wool.

I'll make you a woolly coat like mine."
Sheena's lambs combed out some of Sheena's wool
then Sheena set to work with her knitting needles to make the coat.

The coat fitted Huggy a treat.

It was warm and cosy and had shiny brown buttons
made out of conkers.

Huggy thought he looked a super trooper in it!

Huggy wore it all week;
it was just right, but, oh dear one afternoon as he was scuttling through the woods a thread from the coat came loose and caught on a blackberry bramble bush.
The knitting started to unravel.
Huggy was so busy looking for his friends that he didn't notice until nearly all of the coat had disappeared.
All that was left was the neckband and one sleeve!

A family of mice spotted the wool and thought that it would make them a nice soft nest, so they gathered it up and took it home.

Susie Squirrel had been watching from her tree.
She called out to Huggy, but it was too late; all the wool had gone.

"No problem Huggy," he said. "You shall have the best coat of all, made out of some of the hairs from my tail!"

Huggy thought that a horse-hair coat would be very unusual, so with Harold's permission he pulled several handfuls of the long course hairs from Harold's tail.

"I think that Manjit Mouse will be kind enough to weave it into a very good jacket," said Harold.

"He is very handy at making things.
You just tell him what style you would like."

Manjit was a cobbler who usually made shoes,
but he said that it would be no trouble to sew Huggy a coat.
Huggy chose a style of jacket that a soldier might wear.
Manjit even made some pretend medals to go on it as well.

Huggy was thrilled with his soldier's coat.
He marched up and down saying "left right, left right,"
until his brother and sister got fed up with him.

The first day, the coat was very comfy;
the second day it tickled a bit; the third day it was itchy;
but by the fourth day it had become very scratchy and he had to take it off.

Harold saw how upset Huggy was about this,
so he told Manjit what had happened.

Manjit, being a very kind mouse, suggested that he could make Huggy
a nice soft jacket with a hood out of some of the scraps of leather
that he had left over from people's shoes.

Huggy thought that a leather coat would be very trendy,
so Manjit took some measurements and started
to sew the coat right away.

When it was finished Hugggy tried it on.
He thought that he looked very handsome in it.
He turned this way and that way looking at his reflection in the mirror.

He showed his coat to Dr Raj and nurse Kerrie at the hospital
when he had his last special medicine.
They both thought that the leather coat was the smartest of all.

Huggy wore his leather coat all of the time because it was comfortable.
It didn't fall apart like the moss coat.
It didn't get any holes in it when he went to bed like the silk cloak.
It didn't come unravelled when it caught on a blackberry bramble bush
like his lovely woolly coat.
And, it wasn't scratchy like his horse-hair soldier coat.

But... after a while something strange seemed to be happening.
The soft leather material started getting spots.
The spots grew into bumps that were a bit itchy.
Whatever could it be?

Mummy took Huggy's coat off, and guess what?
The little bumps on Huggy's coat were really his spines starting to grow back.
How excited he was.
Mummy cuddled him and said that he had been a brave little hedgehog
and that soon he wouldn't need a coat as in a little while
he would have all of his spines back again.

Huggy didn't have to go back to the hospital every day now;
only once a month for his special medicine, but he did have to remember
to take his "get better soon" tablets every day.

To ride on Harold's back as he galloped about the field...

...and to play marbles with Manjit mouse's children.

Huggy felt much better now.

Sometimes he was a bit tired and would have a lie down, but he decided that he now had the best coat of all!

Mummy gave a big party for all the animals, Dr Raj and nurse Kerrie to say thank you for being so kind in helping her little boy to get better.